PAPERBACK POETS Second Series 3: Robert Gray

CREEK
WATER
JOURNAL

Robert Gray

University of Queensland Press

Published by University of Queensland Press, St. Lucia,
Queensland, 1974
© Robert Gray, 1974

Printed and bound by Peninsula Press Ltd., Hong Kong
Designed by Cyrelle

Distributed in the United Kingdom, Europe, the
Middle East, Africa, and the Caribbean by Prentice-Hall
International, International Book Distributors Ltd., 66
Wood Lane End, Hemel Hempstead, Herts., England.

Acknowledgements: *Makar, New Poetry, Poetry Australia,
Transit.* Seven of these poems first appeared in different
form in *Introspect, Retrospect* (1970), published by
Lyre Bird Writers.

*National Library of Australia
Cataloguing-in-Publication data*

Gray, Robert, 1945 —
    Creekwater journal/ [by] Robert Gray. — St. Lucia, Q.:
University of Queensland Press, 1974. — (Paperback
poets. Second series; 3).
ISBN 0 7022 0945 7.
ISBN 0 7022 0935 X Paperback.

    I. Title. (Series)

A821.3

Contents

Journey: the North Coast

Next thing, I wake up in a swaying bunk,
as though aboard a clipper at sea,
and it's the train, that booms and cracks,
it tears the wind apart.
Now the man's gone
who had the bunk below me. I swing out,
cover his bed and rattle up the sash —
there's sunlight teeming
on the drab carpet. And the water sways
solidly in its silver basin, so cold
it joins together through my hand.
I see from where I'm bent
one of those bright crockery days
that belong to so much I remember.
The train's shadow, like a bird's,
flees on the blue and silver paddocks,
over fence posts that seem split from stone,
and banks of fern,
a red clay bank, full of roots,
over a dark creek, with logs and leaves suspended,
and blackened tree trunks.
Down these slopes move, as a nude descends a staircase,
the slender white gum trees,
and now the country bursts open on the sea —
across its calico beach, unfurling;
strewn with flakes of light
that make the whole compartment whirl.
Shuttering shadows. I rise into the mirror
rested. I'll leave my hair
ruffled a bit that way — and fold the pyjamas,
stow the book and wash bag. Everything done,

press down the latches into the case
that for twelve months I've watched standing out
of a morning, above the wardrobe
in a furnished room.

Kangaroo

That hungry face
moves on grass
the way an artist's pencil
retouches
shadows.

Then, when he's bounding
head borne
refined as a deer's, relaxed
before a powerful
tight basketball attack.

And the toe-nail, in the fore-front,
a stevedore's claw
(tears with it, cantilevered on his tail);
those forepaws
of a house-dog begging.

So that here, sitting up and simply,
is the unknown
energy, which is nature,
that's able to spawn, as one,
every extreme thing.

The hospital

All day I've escaped within this book.
Now, dusk comes
soaking slowly into the compartments
of the high, bare window.
And I lie down inside these immaculate strong sheets,
where I am going to be
a long
time. From one of the other dimly-
lighted beds, that are drifting with me
through these days, the faint
sounds of a wireless. And a nurse
flickers by
out in the corridor; that squeaking
vinyl. There are tea trays,
somewhere near. Beyond the window's crucifix
comes Venus —
a star like thistledown.
Church bells have begun ringing, far off,
on the dark clouds,
and I hear the sounds of children, running about late,
down somewhere in the grass,
and swings creaking.
I realize that it's been, outside, a bright hot day.

The farm woman speaks

Winter has arrived, the winds scour this place.
Giving the children broth,
I show them now, through the dull windows,
trees rocked by a cruel cough.

We can't take a bad year,
and the lino looks like an over-ripe banana;
there's no help pacing the floors.
Leaves are scuttling on the verandah

from those trees that boom all day. Usually
you don't notice the trees' noise until night,
but if you wake then, you'd swear the sea had come
crashing inland; that awful fright

passes as you realize
where you really are, and where we are
is with crops burnt by frost, the cows
eating dry cornstalks, with all of our care

about three children and the little money
sunken here; with the pasture grass
of a morning, in this worst season for years,
thick with crushed glass —

Of a morning, I see him let the gates fall open.
The moon thaws. Wind floats bubbles
out of a magpie — and bears upon a salver
the croak of the crows.

He jerks in boots towards the shed,
buckets pulling at his neck.
A fig tree is clenched upon the earth, and strain
bulges its tendons. The fences sag.

There are still the times when he will turn to me.
At night, I drowse by the persimmon of the logs,
and, first, he puts an arm around me —.
Only, those flames then feel like a striding flag.

Landscape 1

Grey
suburban daybreak
like a newspaper
photo

through the wire
of the used car lot, over
the closed faces
of houses, that are packed here

ordered
as a switchboard.
And in this light, the lone
outstanding thing

the dark
poplar —
making this the photo of
an explosion,

an uprush of earth that's
clotted, not with leaves but
with clods, with
boulders.

Organic, it seems that violent —
Against this now
fluorescent
dawn.

Church grounds

Bright Sunday at lunchtime
in the grimy suburb:
the presbytery's at prayers
or eating, and the nuns also —
I shortcut through
their schoolyard, down the steps
beside the church, onto
asphalt marked out
for basketball, in orange,
with the metal goals
swung down by the kids, the nets
torn and hanging like
stranded seaweed.
The garbage cans are tipped over
by them or
the stray dogs. Down here
under brick walls
(the colour of cold baked meat)
a flock of pigeons
walking. Nothing else around.
The pigeons pedal off in all
directions, eyes backwards — they
keep pecking
at the air in front of them
as they go. Tick, tick, tick.
If they're not
stabbing at the ground
for crumbs, they're keeping on
into nothing;
that's their whole life . . .

"Scattered lights"

Scattered lights,
one pub, and one garage.
Driving through
in the woodsmoke dusk.
A culvert
at the town limits;
the road goes on, straight,
fading. The flat
grey heath
disappearing close, on either side.
This blustery wind
brings rain — just
short hairs
on a barber's sheet,
marking the windscreen.

Morning

Feeding chickens, pollard scattered like wet sand.

— Jump down stolidly from their roost
as an old sailor jumps
with his peg-leg;
underneath half a corrugated iron tank,
open ended.

I'm stepping around the bare black ground;
wire-netting propped
with lopped poles.
Moss about, bits
of brick poking through and
bones. Rusted wrench
pressed into the ground, jaws open:
a tyrannosaurus head. Reeds.

In packing cases, one side gone, the eggs
in dry grass;
on this cold morning, they're warm, smooth:
Surprising stone

almost weightless.
Bent over;
at the side of my face
the silver, liquid paddocks; steam.
My eyes and nose are damp, I see through my own smoke.

Finding the eggs, dry — the colour of dry sand.

"Outside"

Outside, the long wet verandah boards
with leaves blown in.

Where else could our souls live,
but on the earth.

Landscape 2

Thumping of the waves.
I walk, slide
subside
on the sides of
in amongst
the sandhills —
out of sight of the sea.
Here stings
like insects, on bare legs;
it's white, dry, and
lit by
a wintry sun.
The raw smell
of ocean
on such gusty day,
a throat ache.
Amongst the tangle
of beach vines, the juicy plump pig-face
in purple bloom.
                        The sand's
mottled with grey
weeds, dry and clicking,
with sulphurous
blady grass.
There are skitterings:
                        lizards
and things
that escape with a crackle.
I make for the railway line
wading
in dead grass, matted

like an old dried mop;
using a stick.
Then walking between the rails on
sleepers, shale;
the smell is soaked oil.
Either side, as though covered in ash,
brandishing leaf and cone
weapons, the banksias
corroboree.
And hear
now
a bell-miner —
that lightest hammering
upon
      (a light metal thing
      made bounce on)
metal: say on
this satin, polished
line. — Its
        ding ding   ding ding ding

Back there

Farmer in a brittle morning
struggling with the solid milk cans,
his gasping all about him —

Across the yard
of scarred mud,
the tangled branches
iron lace,
and the shed is going down sideways
under convolvulus.

There's moss
on the walls
one side of the house.
A rusty plough
stranded, like the horns of a
twisted neck,
out in the mouldy
grass —

And over the raw, stripped paddocks, up
on
the windy skyline,
the children run,
capering
all about that huge nerve-end,
a bare tree:
flickering, black.

Salvation Army hostel

I'm woken up — and God knows
what's the time. It's
a woman screeching, over there
the other side of
the light-well.
I strained against the window-wire, tonight, and saw
the bottom, with rotting rag,
cardboard — a no-man's
greenish hole. And there's
evidently been rain,
surprisingly — the aftermath still
falling from a
broken gutter somewhere,
onto
that concrete
way down —
a clattering. No . . .
she's yelling at someone
on a floor above this who's
taking a piss, out his window —
It keeps on. He must have
got a flagon in
this place, and have his cock out through
the criss-cross
grille. A dripping
now, past me — turned over so's
to listen. I can almost see
his blind, bloated face up there
gasp.
No one else but that woman
seems awake. Who suddenly drags her window down. —

15

Both gone.
And I lie in the stiff, thin,
stencilled sheets,
again. Like an unresolved equation;
in this aperture.

18 poems

A waterbird goes up
out of dead grass, with that slow flight —
its wings, the water lapping.

This chair, made of frayed light —
it speaks of absence
like half a carpenter's join.

Dusk. I go to scythe
under the trees at the front gate —
The pale moths rising.

In the rock pool, grass
moves with the water. The violin bows
of an orchestra, *adagio*.

Folding these sacks
over in the shed. From the house,
the sound of crockery.

In the lane where I pass,
someone walks back with a scrap of bush,
not glancing up, at dusk.

The rain: white grapes.
And this cobweb odour of
the wet dust.

I put the milk-bottle on the doorstep,
a little tap-water inside —
it reveals the moonlight in the same
frail quarter as this overlooked moon.

Those trees, blue parsley;
I'm walking back late, over the golf course.
I have no need to hurry.

The back fence is falling —
or it's lifted within a Hokusai wave —
the morning-glory vine.

The molten globe
in the sunset, tremulous as a drop of
water about to fall.

These ripe days,
the heat, the tenderness;
a white bathtub filled with green water,
the leaves against the glass.

A few cars, away off
on the freeway, over wide fields —
a lost burst of tracer fire
through the bright afternoon.

Eye-watering glare;
even those rocks are rusted,
barbed seawater.

On this peak, alone;
in the wind, it feels as if my shirt
is trying to go back.

Sultry night. The moon
is small and fuzzy, an aspirin
in a glass of water.

These chairs and tables —
such Egyptian gestures, of deference,
have filled our houses.

Smokestack, evening sky;
and the smoke, a woman's long hair
as she pauses underwater.

On climbing the Stone Gate Peak

(Hsieh Ling-yün, 385–433 A.D.)

In a floating gown, I have come among these
           promontories alone;
the path is struggling on like a wounded snake.
The crags above Stone Gate are piled one upon the other:
it seems that they must topple from amongst the rushing
           mist.
All about on ledges cling the twisted pines;
all over the rocks there is moss, like a discoloured snow.
I wander into a dark copse, which the late sun pierces,
and in this gloom, a pool of scarlet water.
I have left behind the haunts of the ape and deer;
only a bird now mournfully crying out, in search of its
           mate.
I climb by caves where dripping water rings like crystal,
and the leaves of dwarf bamboo are dripping.
It is because of the waterfall thrown down, around here,
           on stones:
the splintering of a white jade staff.
I watch how that long pole of water goes on shattering —
it is no more diminished than Liu-hai with age.
Across the vibrating pool, a light smoke is windborne,
and drifts above me: the spirit of a great bird.
I climb again, breaking the cobwebs of mist;
vines are trailing from the cliff beneath which I find
           my way.
And then, coming from a crevasse, gaze towards
           other mountains:
they are blue and green inks, allowed to run upon slanted
           silk.

How could one live among these mountains, but with the
        True Mind,
that asks for nothing and yet is open to all that is?
For such rugged peaks do not prolong one gentle
        configuration,
and yet I find the strange flowers (that are struck like an
        instrument).
Only one who knows Detachment, and lets his thoughts
        grow still,
could love these mountains, since his mind is
        unconcerned.

The pine

With a snow-cap
only
of needles;
aslant. And the lopped-off
branches of
various lengths
about its trunk.
The rhythm amongst these
such
a music, all
by chance.
Alone
in the back paddock
in the yellow grass.

Early to rise

For a while, I'm still warm from your bed;
or too intent listening
to every sound
to feel the cold.
Outside, it is a drizzly dawn.
I creep down the driveway,
boots under-arm —
socks getting soaked.
I had brought you home, and
step over the front gate now,
offering my undefended back — gone
beneath the trees in your street.
Hurry to the station,
arms pushed down in my overcoat, head soaked.
I stand on the platform with the cracked faces
of the early shift,
workmen herded
like cows for milking, and
think about
the smell of your body, under those blankets,
warm
as fresh bread. Your whispering.
These men
squint up, with their collars about them,
from under the awning,
at rain whirling
like sparks. Grey sky, grey shapes
of trees — fish skeleton
shapes — faint blocks, and faint
chimney-spire.
I stand about, trying not to shake;

an Aeroplane Jelly mirror
in which to, surreptitiously, rearrange
my glued-together hair.
The train comes, sliding along
the platform's edge. We get in;
they don't seem to speak a word to one another.

The death of Ronald Ryan

(February 3, 1967)

In the crash
pigeons on the
roof whirr
up, clattering
of wings —
visible
to the pickets
beyond
those walls, who
slowly
are
at that signal
turned
around. It's done.
Grey
as Lancashire:
deserted
iron galleries.
— A revolving like a punchbag.
The dusty skylights
receive
early thin yellow
sun.
The tower clock
's nine o'clock dong,
clang
of the trap and
his mind went flying
in that sound,
and from such tensed

sling.
To echo?
What has been done?
Some birds settling down
later
along the way back.
— Hey there's no air here
in this bag!
You don't want to see me —
Those pigeons
in the gravel of the
roadside
are taking hasty steps, puffed
and
eyeing us side-
ways with
eyes trembling.

Landscape 3

A flowering peach tree
wind's blown
down.
— The branches curve
in a brandy balloon
shape — although, seem more
a suppliant
attitude, with their diagonal
slant.
And suspended all about,
heavy
glistening white
blossoms. Thick
masses on the limbs, they
fly
at the furthest tips.
— It is a wave, shattering;
driven spray!

"I'm sitting inside"

I'm sitting inside
from the door. A shirt of mine's
hung on the line
in the rain.

And that rain keeps on
steadily
drifting. I can see it
against the dark
tree trunk,
like a movie screen
flicker.

And in the rain
a bedsheet
is also pegged
up, unevenly, along that
sagging
line.

It's there,
patient
and heavy as
a rhinoceros
in whitewash.

Within the traveller's eye

A late afternoon. From this passing train
one sees the forest.
It is like a cupboard, in some deserted room,
with its door ajar.

There has been rain. Now the sunlight reappears
late in the day.
We are flying low, through these small country towns . . .

Morning glory vines grow over the wire fences
in the shape of huge snowdrifts.
Someone fat is leaning heavily on his verandah rail.

And those old pine trees in a loose main street,
where sparrows live like fleas.

We go above the mud and fallen light of an estuary;
a few of the birds arise.
The river, towards evening, is moving slowly
under the slow sky.

Seeing these small towns, it brings to mind
the lives of old women.

There are the lavatories, out in those back yards
overgrown with paspalum.
The wet cardboard box, lying about.
The piles of weathered palings stacked on trestles.

And a floorcloth, that the dog has taken.

There's always this shallow afternoon light.

The steep iron roofs on these wood places;
they face each other in the blue metal side streets,
with their open drains out of which the grass stands,
and a wood ramp across to each.

There is a utility moving
behind tall roadside heads of grass,

a child's white apron.

And a man is walking on the long shadows
of the telegraph poles, going for cigarettes and matches
to the shop.

I know the dim, unused sitting rooms:
a faint gleam over the lino
and everything in there as rounded
as Melba's bodice.
The fringes on everything.

In those houses is the smell of boiled vegetables,
and of something else —
it is the sexual hatreds, stored away
like china or cuff links,
that will never be spoken.

As the daylight is turned down low
in the grass, the people by their kitchen windows,
or in the outside bathroom
at the end of the verandah,
can hear the frogs

and crickets
begin, out in those flat, soggy paddocks.

But we have gone out miles beyond a town.
The shadow of the tallest mountain
in the valley wall

is lengthening over the empty plain of grass
we move across.

And it feels that if you continue to watch
you will see this shadow indicate, like a finger,
a grave, lying open,
somewhere there.

But you do not try to turn your face away.

23 poems

Sanding the floorboards;
across the house, in the blank window,
hibiscus flowers.

A broken umbrella
standing like a spider, in the sleet
on the drifting canal.

The first of autumn . . .
I've been getting along without you;
now, a touch of fear.

On the enamel dish, slice open
this pear;
rain hangs in the window gauze.

Late afternoon.
Clouds that make you think of Kilimanjaro
from the dry savanna.

Even a scrape of leaves
on the concrete . . . I think that's
the touch of her sandals, again.

Soaking in the hot bath;
on a radio somewhere
the time-pips. — It's three o'clock.

I get up and go to the window;
bright moonlight —
the sea is a glass that's brimming
under the tap.

Some children's voices,
a piano, in the hollow School of Arts.
In the alley, rain floating.

A hot night; I go into the garden.
I try to tighten the tap, but it keeps dripping
on the brick. Mosquitoes come around.

Stone jug filled
with milk — and these two bubbles
like an igloo.

The factory window deals
(as people cross) its cards of daylight.
I know I'll have to lose.

Passing on a train;
bedsheets borne out from a clothes-line
and the pasture-land.

Huge, glittering stars.
Looking up, out among the frogs'
croaking, croaking.

A porch with lattice;
the green tendrils are moving
in front of the surf.

The dragonfly revolves
on the spot, slacks, shoots-off, glides; the
movements like an ice-yacht.

Sitting indoors —
the hens in the blazing yard
creak like a hinge.

The rain, soft and everywhere . . .
it becomes the cricket calls
crackling, popping, in the loam.

Walking in high forest;
a swallow   blown away
from a crest in the dirt road.

In the city,
the unexceptional night —
small change.

A drop hung,
indoors, from the tap's blunt
beak. A bird sings.

The rain comes at night —
swipe of the puma.

Burnt-out cornstalks askew
in the wet.—
Standing hooded with a hessian sack
amongst a battle's aftermath
long ago.

Credo

What shall we believe in? Here,
it's a stone

because you cannot think this away.
Or the polished table —

across it, light from the window falls.
Leaves outside
are moving, deep within this light.

"The world is independent of my will."

40

A labourer

He goes out early, before work, half asleep,
webs of frost on the grass; wading
paspalum to the wood-heap,
a bone-smooth axe handle pointing at him. It lifts the
            block
on a corner of beetled, black
earth. The logs are like rolled roasts,
they tear apart on red-fibred meat. The axe squeaks out.
Lifting it —
the head pulls backwards —
now he sinks to where he is. And the new tile roofs
encroaching about
in the thin water of the sun;
the lavatories towards here, up the back yards.
Roosters scream
through iron, spurred timber
left stand. Bringing it down
bounces gong-blows off the ground, raises the crows;
forging off with rusted cries
into the steam. He takes an armful of the kindling
to drop in the box beside the stove,
and small splinters hang
from a red, hieroglyphed hand —
These for the child, who's father to this man;
sitting, so reluctantly,
in the small mist of his breakfast.

41

Boarding house poems

1

The landlord
standing on bare feet
saws
at the bread
in the middle of a Saturday
afternoon.
A nasal
racing commentator's voice.
His wife
holding a cigarette
in the television room.
You go back
quietly on the linoleum,
and
closing your door.

2

Sound of traffic
outside, continuously
back and forth —
the table tennis
highway.
A sound
as if some kid
of an afternoon
is swinging viciously
right, and left,
cutting through the air
with a stick;
and a rapid bumping,
slapping noise
over the tar joins
in the concrete.
It's hot.
I lie on top of the bed
with a book.
A clock drips,
and the leaf shapes barely move
on the yellow blind.

3

PUBLIC LIBRARY
Putting a book up, moving on;
keeping hold of the one
pared volume.
Hushed,
starkly fluorescent-lit,
the air
dressed with dust.
A bald man
digs into his nose;
mustachioed man,
dog-like, in a moth-eaten overcoat; the
anxiously-peering woman.

4

Turning away
from the ladies hairdressing salon
atmosphere
of the advertising agency —
go to work where
it's all
factories,
vacant lots, of weed and broken concrete,
terrace houses,
alleys. Down here
a light in the Italian corner shop
burns all day.
Anything feels better
for a while.
And one time
you find yourself in a blunt real agreement
with someone —
that one of the other workers is officious;
"a bloody old woman".
The taste of comradeship.

5

Lunchtimes
you see
from a bank
above the hurricane wire
a schoolboy
soccer match:
the ball
trickling smoke
all about the dry grass;
the tall chimneys
above
trailing their smoke
one way.

6

Going amongst the dark wood
in the hall
early, while it's still afternoon,
you notice
these calico flowers, crowded
in the vase.
How they keep on hoping.

7

Wednesday, the dead, dark
and middle of the week —
hardly redeemed
by its being pay-day;
after putting aside the rent,
straight away this evening
the most urgent job,
the washing to the laundromat.
Reading a novel,
inattentive,
on the orange polythene chair;
parched smell
of dry-cleaning fluid,
and lifeless, dehydrated air
from spin-dryers.
During this hour, and more,
lots of times look up
and find her —
unloading bedsheets
that are like great lumps of dough
from a washing machine, or untangling
heat-blasted things,
holding the door against her side.
Intent profile
and the jeans stretched
tightly around, a
taut weight
in her shirt:
excitement
that rolls over in your stomach like
a dolphin.

And then, nothing more to do, but go,
as her air would indicate.
It's started to rain
lightly.
The rain comes undone
from a rail,
walking beside it home.
The rain is sliding
like a belt,
at an angle through the street light.
With both arms around
the large plastic bag of wash,
feeling it warm
against your body —
and the minute drops
cling
all over your face
and come stirring down, out of
your hair.

Rising like a clear moon,
on the wall
at the foot of my bed,
one picture —
the photograph of
a Buddha;
this alert face with a detachment like the moon's;
with such
relentlessness.
"As Orpheus walked
through the forest, so you have passed
in this world:
a voice that might dispel
the beast in men."
Lying here
I'm reminded, once again,
that it is definitely
askew.

"The single principle of forms"

All day a storm has fermented. Now the clouds are huge above the mountains.

A horse stands in the paddock and swings its wooden face at the flies.

It stands with one hind-leg poised lightly by the other, like the way a male ballet dancer stands.

Its muzzle soggy as the stump of a freshly-cut banana palm.

And that coarse long tail makes you think of an Indian, waiting with a tomahawk amongst the forest.

The horse trembles its flank in the heat, and now the lightning shudders —

The silverish lightning, over those great haunches of cloud.

The meat works

Most of them worked around the slaughtering
out the back, where concrete gutters
crawled off
heavily, and the hot, fertilizer-thick,
sticky stench of blood
sent flies mad,
but I settled for one of the low-paid jobs, making mince
right the furthest end from those bellowing,
sloppy yards. There, the pigs' fear
made them mount one another
at the last minute. I stood all day
by a shaking metal box
that had a chute in, and a spout,
snatching steaks from a bin they kept refilling
pushing them through
arm-thick corkscrews, grinding around inside it, meat or
                    not —
chomping, bloody mouth —
using a greasy stick
shaped into a penis.
When I grabbed it first time
it slipped, slippery as soap, out of my hand
in the machine
that gnawed it hysterically a few moments
louder and louder, then, shuddering, stopped;
fused every light in the shop.
Too soon to sack me —
it was the first thing I'd done.
I had to lug gutted pigs
white as swedes
and with straight stick tails

to the ice rooms, hang them by their heads
on hooks. Or fill a long intestine
with sausage meat.
You got meat to take home —
bags of blood;
red plastic with the fat showing through.
We'd wash, then
on the blue metal
towards town; but after sticking your hands all day
in snail-sheened flesh,
you found, around the nails, there was still blood.
I didn't usually take the meat.
I'd walk home on
the shiny, white-bruising beach, in mauve light,
past the town.
The beach, and those startling, storm-cloud mountains,
            high
beyond furthest fibro houses, I'd come
to be with. (The only work
was at this Works.) — My wife
carried her sandals, in the sand and beach grass,
to meet me. I'd scoop up shell-grit
and scrub my hands,
treading about
through the icy ledges of the surf
as she came along. We said that working with meat was
            like
burning-off the live bush
and fertilizing with rottenness,
for this frail green money.
There was a flaw to the analogy
you felt, but one
I didn't look at, then —
the way those pigs stuck there, clinging onto each other.

Landscape 4

The river at its brim —
vast sweep
of ripples, full sailed in morning sun.

Clotted, drip-leafed gums
lean on the red
mud bank. Rickety log jetty
in socks
of oyster shells,
where milk cans stand.

The sawmill, a roof of rusty tin
on posts, over
shadow. The diagonal wooden
crane beam.

And dunes of sawdust lying about;
from somewhere there
a giant cigarette smoke.

The farmer, in felt hat, rides
a tractor, rakes up the dust —
lurches
on a wading animal. Huge embossed wheels
roll down.

The exhaust-pipe chimney
beside him: through those clear fumes
and heat, the mountains —

each a half-pitched
Big Top,
blue-black —
as if seen through a window
awash.
That stripe
of lacquered green cane.

Let off on the highway,
I climb down,
heaving a haversack
through smoky green bushes,
sulphur
bladey grass. The thrashing noise
behind. Insects everywhere, on the boil.
Stinking Roger —
hot, sweetish, fermenting smell.

And the river
here, in this mid-morning's
littered
with a whole street of
fallen plate glass,
filled with
light.

The cats

While my wife gets ready for work, I stay under the blankets on the couch, where I sleep when I've worked late.

The radio's muffled thumping, dishes' clatter. She goes, calling out about the shoe polish — swirl around of shoulder-bag and hair, to smile again from the door.

Dressed, I walk in the back yard, and the autumn air is thin, the sky washed and shiny, like a squeaky windowpane.

These two camphor laurels, stirring back and forth, a sound like the edge of the surf. Their leaves glitter — the running water of the shallows.

And the shuddering of the expressway, above all the red tile roofs.

When I go around the front to collect the garbage can, there are cats about: I shout and stamp. They've been mating at night here, making a horrible noise, like a baby's desperate crying. It wakes my wife, who lost her child at birth.

I don't make her any promises, now, about that.

Every time I see the cats, I yell and bend to pick up a stone, and they leave with long stalking strides, bellies dragging.

A glass of orange juice. On the breakfast table, this folder of weak advertising puns.

I'm going to go to work late. I eat some toast, standing in the yard; the honey runs back on my hand.

Then cleaning up. As I lift the clothes from where I slept, catch a glimpse out the door — the back part of a cat is ambling by, stealthy and confident. It walks like an Apache's horse.

Poem

Against the old tin
fence these few
weeds

or bushes
forked
and black

long cracks
down a stone
wall

and the pellet-blast
about each
of their leaves

amongst which has come
flying
the panic of all

the small creatures
a rattle of
thin rain

Bright day

The fantail is tying
loosely
a complex knot,
as if as an illustration,
about one spot
in the air

and then drawing it sharp;
yanked-tight
noose
on some frailer string —
the tangled line
in the sun
of a beetle, or other living thing;

throttling it.
It chops that end
short, and
this fantail, with its mantilla —
the swirling,
a blur —
goes off once more, taut;
not far

Again,
like some applause-igniting
artistry,
it flourishes a
variation
of this elaborate bow —

is adding, everywhere,
its satin
finishing touches to the morning.

To the Master, Dōgen Zenji

(1200–1253 A.D.)

Dōgen came in and sat on the wood platform,
all the people had gathered
like birds upon the lake.

After years, had come back from China,
and he'd brought no scriptures — he showed them
empty hands.

This was Kyoto,
at someone-else's temple. He said, All that's important
is the ordinary things.

Making the fire
to boil some bathwater, pounding rice, pulling the weeds
and knocking dirt out of their roots,

or pouring tea — those blown scarves
a moment, more beautiful than the drapery
in paintings by a Master.

— "It is this world of the *dharmas*
(the atoms)
which is the Diamond."

*

Dōgen received, they say, his first insight
from an old cook at some monastery
over there,

who was hanging about on the jetty
where they docked — had come down
to buy mushrooms,

among the rolled-up straw sails,
the fish-nets, and those brocade litters,
geese in baskets.

High sea-going junk,
shuffling and dipping
like an official.

Dōgen could see
an empty shoreline, the pinewood plank of the beach,
the mountains

far-off
and dusty. Standing about
with his new smooth skull.

And horses' lumpy hooves clump on those planks,
they arch their necks
and dip their heads like swans,

manes blown about
like the white threads up from off
the falling breakers,

and holding up a hoof as though it were tender,
the sea grabbing at
the timber below.

— So the two got talking,
the old man told him, Up there,
that place —

the monastery a cliff-face
in the shadowy hill —
My study is cooking;

no, not devotion, not
the sacred books (which was Buddhism). And Dōgen
irate —

he must have thought
who is this old prick, so ignorant
of the Law,

and it must have shown:
Son, I regret
that you haven't caught on

to where it is one discovers
the Original Nature
of the mind and things.

*

Dōgen said, Ideas
from reading, from people, from a personal bias,
toss them all out —

Discolourations.
You shall only discover by looking in
this momentary mind.

And said, The Soto school
isn't one
of the many entities of Buddhism,

you should not even use this name
Soto.
It is just sitting in meditation;

an awareness, with no
clinging to,
no working on, the mind.

Such *zazen* began a long time
before Buddha,
and it will continue forever.

— And upon this leaf one shall cross over
the stormy sea,
among the dragon-like waves.

Evening

In the bus, this silver pole trickling from the hands that have held it.

The bus climbs back like a cockroach onto the Heights. As its gears grind down, people shift themselves, and the conversations fail.

They crush cigarette butts, or screw the ticket into stiff string for poking at their teeth. And with the window open, look out through the thick glass of their own expressions.

Ash falls like dandruff, and that grey smoke vanishes like someone's hair.

There is a woman with wax legs that are melting, running down in blue lumps. A man struggling to his feet drags cruelly at the cord.

Reading the race form or the lottery. A headline says someone-or-other DEAD.

Tonight in these red brick villas, how many headaches like the heat lightning?

The moon shall pass over all these roofs, leaving here a snail's path.

But after the heat of today, there will be a breeze; the sound of a garden hose in the leaves outside. When these people are lying down, beached in their chairs, with legs apart.

And they shall see the curtains set sail, of a sudden, as if for the New World.

27 poems

A train is passing above;
in the pawnbroker's
we can't speak.

You forgot the flowers,
I have kept them in a jar of water.
It smells as if you were here.

Girl laughing in the 'phone,
sitting up on the ledge, legs crossed.
The glass wriggles with rain.

I'm getting up later —
these stormy nights of autumn.
Sailboats on the lake.

4 a.m.; the Milky Way
is blown along, high over the forest.
A truck changes down.

In the locker room
a shower that keeps on slapping . . .
all the sodden newspaper.

A daytime movie,
and coming outside again, it's dark.
I choose the opposite direction.

Rainy weather,
with the light on all day.
Like waiting for someone.

Weary, I tear open the shopping.
From the newspaper waddles
on the table
            like an irate duck
this melon.

So hot, that sparrow looks ill;
sitting on the tap handle.

Freewheeling on a bike —
the butterflies of sunlight
all over me.

Lean in the wash-up, trying out a poem.
On the dark window, the scratches of soft rain.

Heat! From the highway
a willow is seen to move
like a water-weed.

Wake disheveled:
a fly's stumbling and bumping around.
The first light.

Hiking in the bush alone.
All afternoon, through the branches,
vapour trail of a jet.

The pleasure of weeds:
to see them underneath the street-lights.

I thought it was rain beginning
and sat up in the dark to listen —
it must have only been falling leaves.

Using the egg-beater.
Passing, she rests a hand on mine:
"Try harder now."

Sunday morning, late,
wandering to the bathroom, you find
it's filled with sunlight.

Drinks at a bubbler —
but that tear in his filthy trousers
hangs like a mouth.

The train's halted
nowhere. Small birds whirling up
from the dry grass.

Dust-grains on the glass door
in sunlight. Through there
a young girl's wrists, about the vase.

In the heat, dragging myself about.
For the first time, a nun is a person.

Feel my way slowly to the bathroom, then
standing there, suddenly
a clattering in the toilet bowl!

Drunk last night; waking up
with limbs scattered about the bed —
The shiny leaves are moving.

Sunken grave, rusty iron;
come upon, trampling through long grass.
Rain-drop slips down.

A melon, overlooked
out in the muddy paddocks —
it's alright.

The sawmill shacks

The shacks overgrown on the mountainside
we come rattling around
in Ted's bomb — a dirt road,
metal clang
under the car; the trail
to a waterfall.
Silent, cold
bush below,
the tree-tops tattered,
smoke-blue; high,
shot-to-pieces shapes on the frail
winter sky. Halfway
on this cold
volcano, as steep
as sawdust
under a chute, once, in the dead
(oil-dirt and rusty cog)
crawled-through town.
At the top of the dry creek-bed of the street,
a furnace; rusted
cone with a round
tip, its sieve-like
smoke vent. An old Chev
timber truck's sunk
like a bullock down, almost gone,
blind.
The stores and shacks
are shingled weatherboard,
lines scored,
their boards curling
away. Huge, moist ferns

sprout through the boardwalks and
fungus is spreading everywhere, like bright
dried apricot.

Just out, above the road,
the Community Hall,
salmon-pink, slipping
through weed, some planks held by
one nail.
Inside,
boarded-up gloom, dust
in this door-beam
on the breathless floor,
furry.
A hollowness,
splattered with bird-lime. There's
a book on the floor, flaked
to rusty shale,
Baroness Orczy,
"property of
the C.W.A." And a Sunday school print
on the wall: a saint bestowing
rhetorical blessing,
smouldering, through the nicotine-coloured
stain.
A piano, with the seeming grin
of old bones:
caries, and the teeth's
enamel gone . . .

You hear the rudimentary violin,
the stamping boots,
and a sudden dog-like yelp;

tea cups scrape.
The whining, dogmatic women's voices,
and their squawks;
the bellowing, out of florid jowls. Those songs
of a place they've never seen
they called home . . .

Gladys, Clarrie, Madge and Arthur;
concerned about
the hint
of a slight —
or this mind, too often,
a knocked-over
hive;
with so little to do, anywhere here,
but work,
their lives become a long time;
women who'd cry
without finding any tears,
who startled themselves, wondering where this was;
those men
who did not pause at twilight,
whose solution was to put on
a snarl:
people the same as any,
blown away
out of this stony, slanted gap.
They have got lost again, somewhere.
On your mouth
a taste of pity, thinking of us.

And above, these rafters are clotted with nests,
and, treading about,
from inside the piano

74

dead animal stench. You have to push out,
under cobwebs
(the door-screech), stepping
jerkily in thin sun. And a crow lurches away
slides down
far off
we soar
over the vague blue mountainside . . .
How the tree-tops there
like wave crests
glint
in these last, reaching,
spatulate beams. And this huge dome

of air;
navy-blue, porous; the
blue of endless-
ness.
Inside your chest, you feel yourself arising —
Other mountains
far along from here, like skyscrapers
at dusk
with all of their lights out,
in the faint mist.
This opened-up
melon, of the evening.

And here,
the long grasses
are swirled
loosely
as a buoy.
And now the stars,

the first few,
clear
as water
on a grass blade,
appearing
effortless
as stars appear . . .

But we catch ourselves standing about; it is
a sound of water
underneath the crashing of this
tethered avalanche —
the piled-up
heights of the forest —
everywhere.
And all that trickling water
seems an evil sound, in this place:
speaks of
black, icy leaf-mulch
that it sinks through; and spreading over bald, slimy
                    ground
of the roots
standing out, furry, from frozen soil
like rib-cages;
a
deranged scrawl
of sharp-toothed lantana
where only it can pass —
in the enormous day-long gloom;
these torrential lines
of forest.

As if in a ballet
all the light has fallen out of the sky;
and cold rears up;

the wind rises from the left.
Hard to see
the timber-getters' shacks,
each as lightless and empty,
as cast-off,
as a skull; staved-in.
This cold!
It reveals to you, like a disease, the shape of your bones.
Stumble down,
and the headlights swing solidly about
in a dank
cellar of leeches —
Feeling our way
through all four wheels of the car
out
into the long valley.
Dropping here,
among the paddocks upholstered in powdery weeds —
the moon
now fully risen,
afloat
in this immense fine spray
like perfume,
filling all the valley.
And one already knew of nature
it is not "human-hearted";
except, you see that in men it is,
in some men —
and that she has caused it.

North Coast town

Out beside the highway, first thing in the morning,
nothing much in my pockets but sand
from the beach. A Shell station (with their Mens locked),
the closed hamburger stand.

I washed at a tap down beside the changing sheds,
stepping about on mud. Through the wall
smell of that vandals' lavatory,
and the automatic chill flushing in the urinal.

Eat a floury apple, and stand about. At this curb
sand crawls by, and palm fronds here
scrape dryly. Car after car now — it's like a boxer
warming-up with the heavy bag, spitting out air.

And now a car slows, and I run. Two hoods
going shooting. Tattoos and the greasy Fifties pompadour.
Rev in High Street, drop their first can.
Plastic pennants on this distilled morning, everywhere;

a dog trotting, and someone hoses down a pavement;
our image flaps in shop fronts; smoking on
past the pink "Tropicana" motel (stucco, with sea shells);
the RSL, like a fancy-dress Inca; the "Coronation",

a warehouse picture show. We pass
bulldozed acres. This place is becoming chrome,
tile-facing, and plate-glass: they're making California.
Pass an abo, not attempting to hitch, outside town.

The Great Buddha, Kamakura

Great Buddha,
a picture pinned-up behind the door.
All the swooping
loops of his robe;
the dust, twigs and berries,
sparrow droppings.
Crowds.
The Western clothes
wheeling prams, the shouts
of children
with those bright balloons
above their hands.
— Resentment,
idleness,
catching of another's eye,
acidic coins.
These families in the heat.
In every mind
there is its continual argument.
Great Buddha
as high as the leaves —
a flak
of light and shadows.
Smile
elusive as that breeze,
as a day that works out right.

534